Get Moving

Tips on Exercise

by Kathy Feeney

Consultant:
Michael K. Jones, Ph.D., PT
President
American Academy of Health, Fitness, and Rehab Professionals

Bridgestone Books
an imprint of Capstone Press
Mankato, Minnesota

Bridgestone Books are published by Capstone Press
151 Good Counsel Drive, P.O. Box 669, Mankato, Minnesota 56002
http://www.capstone-press.com

Library of Congress Cataloging-in-Publication Data
Feeney, Kathy, 1954–
    Get moving: tips on exercise/by Kathy Feeney.
    p.cm.—(Your health)
    Includes bibliographical references and index.
    ISBN 0-7368-0973-2
    1. Exercise—Juvenile literature. 2. Physical fitness—Juvenile literature. [1. Exercise.
2. Physical fitness.] I. Title. II. Series.
RA781 .F425 2002
613.7—dc21   00-012537

Summary: An introduction to the benefits of exercise, including warming up, drinking water,
    muscle strength, and eating right.

Editorial Credits
Sarah Lynn Schuette, editor; Karen Risch, product planning editor; Linda Clavel,
    designer and illustrator; Jeff Anderson and DeDe Barton, photo researchers

Photo Credits
Capstone Press/Gary Sundermeyer, cover, 1
Comstock, Inc., 4
Gregg R. Andersen, 14, 16, 18
Image Ideas, Inc./Index Stock Photography, Inc., 20
Index Stock Photography, Inc., 10, 12
PhotoDisc, Inc., 6 (lower right inset), 8
Rubberball Productions, 6 (insets)

**Bridgestone Books thanks Rebecca Glaser and Franklin Elementary School, Mankato,
Minnesota, for providing photo shoot locations.**

1 2 3 4 5 6 07 06 05 04 03 02

Table of Contents

Guess What?

Your body has 650 muscles.

Get Moving

Being fit means that your body is healthy and strong. Exercise keeps your body fit. Exercise helps blood and oxygen flow to all parts of your body. Your muscles get stronger when you exercise.

oxygen
a colorless gas found in the air; people breathe oxygen.

The Activity Pyramid

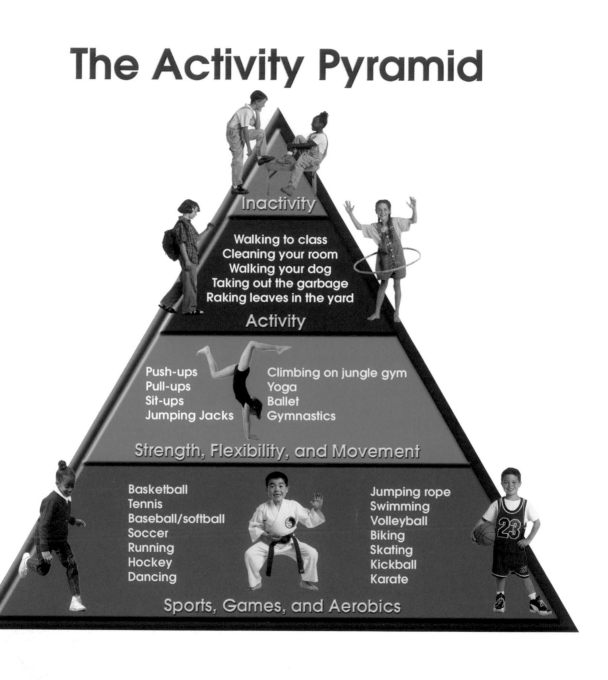

Inactivity

Walking to class
Cleaning your room
Walking your dog
Taking out the garbage
Raking leaves in the yard

Activity

Push-ups
Pull-ups
Sit-ups
Jumping Jacks

Climbing on jungle gym
Yoga
Ballet
Gymnastics

Strength, Flexibility, and Movement

Basketball
Tennis
Baseball/softball
Soccer
Running
Hockey
Dancing

Jumping rope
Swimming
Volleyball
Biking
Skating
Kickball
Karate

Sports, Games, and Aerobics

The Activity Pyramid

You should get different types of exercise every day. The activities near the top of the pyramid help you get moving. The exercises at the bottom help your muscles get stronger.

Guess What?

Your heart is the strongest muscle in your body.

Strong Heart and Lungs

Exercise keeps your heart and lungs strong. Your heart pumps blood through your body. Your heart beats faster when you exercise. Your lungs take in air. Exercise helps fresh oxygen get to your lungs.

Strong Arm Muscles

Exercise makes arm muscles strong. Strong muscles help your arms move. You need strong arm muscles to lift and carry objects. Strong arm muscles help you swim fast or shoot a basketball.

Try This!

Take the stairs instead of riding an elevator. Climbing the stairs is good exercise for your legs.

Strong Leg Muscles

The muscles in your legs help you stand, walk, run, and jump. Your leg muscles need exercise. Exercise gives your leg muscles more power and strength. Strong leg muscles help you snowshoe or skate fast.

Muscle & Exercise Guide
Posterior (Back)

Deltoid
- To Stretch:
  Hold hands behind
  back with arms
  straight. Arm circles.
- To Strengthen:
  Push-ups.

Gluteus Maximus
- To Stretch:
  Knee pull - pull
  knee to chest, lean
  over.
- To Strengthen:
  Squat jumps.
  Walking - climbing.

Gastrocnemius
- To Stretch:
  Hurdle stretch against
  wall.
  Pull on toes with
  knees straight - sitting
  or standing position.
- To Strengthen:
  Toe-heel raisers on
  steps or blocks in 3
  positions;
  toes pointed straight,
  toes pointed in, toes
  pointed out.

Latissimus Dorsi
- To Stretch:
  Hug yourself.
  Sit on floor, pull knees to your
  chest. Roll onto your back and
  up again.
  Roll back with your feet and
  legs over your head - hold.
- To Strengthen:
  Rope climbing without using
  legs. Chin-ups - behind the
  head with arms apart.

Hamstrings
- To Stretch:
  Toe touches - feet spread
  apart, straight legs, touch right
  hand to left toe, left hand to
  right toe. Hurdle sits.
- To Strengthen:
  Squat jumps.

Try This!

Warm up by touching your toes or doing jumping jacks. You should stretch your muscles for at least five minutes before you exercise.

Warming Up

You should warm up before exercise. Warming up gets your muscles, heart, and lungs ready for exercise. It stretches your muscles. Warming up helps you become flexible. You may hurt your body if you exercise before warming up.

flexible
being able to move
and bend easily

Guess What?

You should drink eight glasses of water every day.

Your Body Needs Water

Your body sweats when you exercise.
It is important to replace the water
you lose when you sweat. Drink water
before, during, and after you exercise.
Your body stays cool and your muscles
work better when you drink water.

Eating Right

Your body needs healthy food to work well. Healthy food gives your body nutrients such as vitamins, minerals, and carbohydrates. These nutrients help your body grow. Eating right also gives you the energy to exercise.

nutrient
something that is needed by people, animals, and plants to stay healthy and strong

Fitness Can Be Fun

Many people have fun when they exercise. Listening to music will help make exercise fun. Exercising with your friends also can be fun. Find an activity that you enjoy such as playing on a jungle gym. Keeping your body fit will help you feel good about yourself.

Hands On: Test Your Fitness

You and a friend can try sit-ups to test your fitness. Ask your physical education teacher for other exercises that you can do to test your fitness. Your physical education teacher can also show you the right way to warm up before you exercise.

What You Need

A soft, clean surface such as a gym mat
A friend
Stopwatch

What You Do

1. Lie down on your back on the gym mat.
2. Bend your knees, leaving your feet flat on the ground.
3. Cross your arms over your chest.
4. Keep your elbows close to your chest.
5. Raise the trunk of your body and touch your thighs with your elbows.
6. Lower your back down to the floor.
7. Have your friend start the stopwatch. Do as many sit-ups as you can for one minute.

You should be able to do 12 to 15 sit-ups in one minute.

Words to Know

carbohydrate (kar-boh-HYE-drate)—a nutrient that provides energy

energy (EN-ur-jee)—the strength to be active without getting tired

heart (HART)—a large muscle inside the chest that pumps blood through the body

lungs (LUHNGS)—a pair of organs inside the chest that are used for breathing

mineral (MIN-ur-uhl)—a nutrient found in nature

muscle (MUHSS-uhl)—a part of the body that helps it move; exercise makes muscles strong.

vitamin (VYE-tuh-min)—a nutrient that helps keep people healthy

Read More

Royston, Angela. *A Healthy Body.* Safe and Sound. Des Plaines, Ill.: Heinemann Library, 2000.

Silverstein, Alvin, Virginia Silverstein, and Laura Silverstein Nunn. *Physical Fitness.* My Health. New York: Franklin Watts, 2001.

Internet Sites

BrainPop: Fitness Movie
http://www.brainpop.com/health/growthanddevelopment/ fitness/index.weml

Get Fit! Don't Quit!
http://tqjunior.thinkquest.org/4139

Why Exercise is Cool
http://www.kidshealth.org/kid/stay_healthy/fit/ work_it_out.html

Index